Scotland
in cameracolour

Scotland
in cameracolour

Photographs by F. A. H. BLOEMENDAL

Text by MARGARET HIDES

LONDON

IAN ALLAN LTD

First published 1972
Reprinted 1981

ISBN 0 7110 0316 5

© Ian Allan Ltd 1972

Published by Ian Allan Ltd, Shepperton, Surrey;
and printed in Italy by
Graphische Betriebe Athesia, Bolzano

Introduction

In a cacophonous age Scotland still offers a chance to listen to silence, a possibility uncomprehended, or long since gone, in much of Europe.

In winter and early spring there is the drama of snows on lofty peaks. In May and June the newness of birch and larch diffuses a green mist on the hills. September and early October is the time for high colour, with gold and bronze and heather purple blotched all over the country, as though a modern artist had stood at a great height and flung his paints in free expression, using the whole of Scotland as his canvas. This is a lovely time to be there, and the weather too is often at its best with good visibility.

The Briton seeing Scotland in fair weather becomes easy prey to Chauvinism, convinced that the Mediterranean, and Europe's renowned lake resorts, have nothing to offer except probably some guarantee of fiercer sunshine. Cities and towns seem no more than punctuation marks between endless lochs, moorland, hill ranges, forests and coastal splendour.

Divided into 33 counties, Scotland covers an area of 33,414 square miles, which includes 186 inhabited islands.

Man has almost always been here; there are traces of Stone Age dwellings and Iron Age forts.

The old approach to the Kingdom of Scotland was by the sea. Centuries of border unrest made entry by Edinburgh's port of Leith the surest, safest way to get there, and long after peace came to the Borders people continued to come by the traditional route, even into the early days of the 19th century.

Queen Victoria's first visit to Scotland—the country which was eventually to become so beloved to her and her Consort—was by sea.

The easy, swift road and air approaches rob the modern traveller of unforgettable views of Edinburgh and the east coast as one sails up the Firth of Forth. But the traveller with a car need not feel cheated, especially if he has time to shun the fast motorway and approach by the quieter, straight highway of the A68 where every other signpost seems to point to remains of Hadrian's Wall before the route lifts through the Cheviot Hills and up on to the spectacular brooding high moorlands of Northumbria.

On the Borders—the land whose metaphorical ghosts of ancient border bandits and ruined abbeys inspired many of the novels of Sir Walter Scott—the swift salmon rivers cut through hills to converge on the Tweed; and the sheep whose wool has made that name famous throughout the world are set against a pastoral background.

The panoramas are still mainly agricultural as one moves deeper into the Lowlands where Edinburgh, the country's capital, and Glasgow are the principal cities.

The Lowlands support about two thirds of Scotland's population of five and a quarter million people, and almost all of her industry. Here also, along with the industry, is Loch Lomond and a western seaboard whose scenery is the sort which has a photographer constantly reaching for his camera, desperate to freeze a moment in time with the lonely beauty of waves, distant islands and shadowy hills.

The east coast of the Lowlands has a different flavour. The 20-mile wide peninsula between the Firth of Forth and the Firth of Tay has unique old fishing towns which have managed an unusually happy blend between work-a-day port and holiday resort.

The Scottish Highlands and Islands, covering about a quarter of Britain's land surface, provide the largest area of mountainous and semi-wild land in the whole country.

Less than one in fifty of the population inhabit this part of Britain, leaving its crags and moors to the Golden Eagle, its fast clear rivers to the salmon and trout, its sweeping seascapes and curving headlands to the gannet; the woods and tucked-away glens are the province of red deer, roe deer, wildcat and pine marten.

The true Scot will not refer to any of the high peak ranges—the Cairngorms, the Grampians, the Torridon range, Ben Nevis—as "mountains" but always as "hills".

The Gaelic language survives in some areas of the Highlands. The Shetland islands are nearer to Norway than to many parts of Scotland, and it is in islands like these that old languages survive and where the traveller will always find the tranquil corner whatever the season.

The Western Isles, beyond the Minch the long line of the Hebrides, have a bounty of wide deserted sandy beaches and famous names: Harris, Lewis, Benbecula.

Not all the Islands are in the far north: Skye, Bute, Mull, Eigg and Rum, are among a whole cluster of scenic jewels off the west coast.

Nor are all the Highlands remote. In the Central Highlands there is the soft enchantment of Royal Deeside, where the hills come down to the plains in a mingling of rivers and quiet lochs and lush farmlands grazed by Highland cattle. Beautiful holiday beaches and working ports juxtapose, and fairytale, conical-towered castles are never very far away—over 150 of them. Here the Queen has her summer holiday home, Balmoral Castle, and in September visitors come from far and wide to watch the Braemar Royal Highland Gathering.

The Spey Valley, full of the beauty of the Central Highlands, is one of the loveliest valleys in Scotland. Forests, scented with pine, encroach to the edge of heather moors. Britain's only reindeer herd roams here, ospreys have returned to nest in old castle ruins.

The summer visitor can enjoy pony trekking, canoeing, sailing on the lochs, walking, or testing for a foothold on the Cairngorms, whose granite peaks rise to over 4,000ft. The winter visitor should find the best conditions for winter sports in Britain at Aviemore's multi-million pound year-round holiday complex.

The Grampians make the true geographical division between the Central and Northern Highlands. To their north lies what poets have called "The land of the bens and glens and heroes". The traveller who comes here must expect to be cut down to size, overawed by towering peaks and echoes from long-past battles.

Clouds capriciously hurl across the horizon, hiding the sun, and chilling one minute; bringing sun and warmth the next.

This is a haven for wildlife and, for people who are not cast down by solitude and lowering beauty, there is the joyous freedom of nature and a lack of pollution, fast becoming so difficult to track down.

Here are Fort William with Ben Nevis, Scotland's highest mountain; Glenfinnan, where the Young Pretender, Prince Charles Edward Stuart, raised his standard in 1745. The area round Glenfinnan is rich in the history of the ill-fated Stuarts.

Here, too, is Glencoe, one of Scotland's most celebrated glens, "the glen of weeping", whose scenery touches the spirit with its wild audacious sweeps.

Tiobh Sair Rois—Wester Ross—is a region of legend, history and beauty where the traveller can be alone with the wheeling lapwings of the Beinn Eighe Nature Reserve or the grandeur of the sandstone hills of Torridon.

Farther north is Sutherland, the land of John Buchan, where winds drive in over Cape Wrath. Fewer than seven people per square mile live here compared with 586 for Britain as a whole. Roads, few and far between, are provided with passing places, and rocks more than 600 million years old, rise abruptly, curiously shaped, from green wastelands which are humped with outcrops of smaller rocks.

But Sutherland is not all wilderness; good beaches take the harshness out of a rugged coast, the breeding ground for seals; there are lochs and rivers teeming with trout and salmon. The Kirkaig Falls, the highest in the country, are spectacular in their setting. This is the place where those with the interest, and the patience, may see the Golden Eagle and the wildcat. It is easy to see the red deer and the roe deer for they roam freely in Sutherland.

Finally to John o'Groats, and Dunnet Head, the northernmost point of the Scottish mainland, which is in the county of Caithness. Moonlike inland, it is the awesomeness of seascapes which compels attention here, beaches stretch endlessly along the base of enormous cliffs.

Caithness is steeped in pre-history with the marks of the earliest peoples still evident in the cairns and brochs. The Norse influence lingers still.

Sharing this remoteness are the Queen Mother's centuries old Castle of Mey and the futuristic Dounreay Atomic Reactor.

The visitor to this part of Scotland should try to see something of the interesting Caithness Glass, one of the new industries brought to Highland factories at Wick and surrounding areas. Exciting ideas in design marry the ancient Nordic with space-age shapes.

It is not easy in this modern age of unity to interpret to the non-Scot the difference between the Highlander and the Lowlander. It may not even seem necessary, except that the stranger in Scotland finds the appendage "Highlander" and "Lowlander" used time and again.

The Highlands and Lowlands were divided for centuries by language, outlook and geographical differences. Their emnity was mutual. Even at the beginning of the 18th century a Lowland Scot, obliged to go on business to the Highlands, was quite likely to make his will before setting out.

The Highlands begin immediately above Stirling, but there are those who will insist that to find the true Highlander you must go much farther north, to a line above the Caledonian canal.

Generalisations can be misleading but it is the Highland Scot, still with a strong Celtic streak, who likes to encourage the idea that simply to be a Highlander is virtue in itself. The Lowland Scot, less fey, with two feet firmly on the ground, is more prepared to accept all Scotsmen as equal and draw no distinction.

There *are* differences, but they are subtle, and not likely to be very apparent to the passing traveller who finds he is among a delightful people with many common attributes: sturdy individualism; people who know what they want. They will offer dependable friendship, rarely effusive, never obsequious.

The Scots have long memories, they care deeply for their history and are better at keeping faith with their heroes than are their neighbours over the border.

The rich tapestry of early Scottish history is as closely interwoven with the history of France as with that of England. The Romans made only half-hearted attempts to conquer the Pictish and Celtic settlements, and for a short time in the 2nd century occupied parts of the Lowlands.

By the 6th century Angles and Britons had overrun the south-east and the south-west, and the Scots, who had come from Ireland, were established in Argyll.

The Picts and Scots united in 844, but it was not until the mid-11th century that the Britons and Angles were brought into a Scottish Kingdom. By this time the Normans and the English had also begun to settle in parts of the south of Scotland, and the English language was gaining ground in the Lowlands.

From the 9th century Scotland was victim of raids by Norsemen who occupied the Hebrides until the 13th century and the Orkneys and Shetlands until the 15th century.

Edward I, who came to the English throne in 1272, was the first English monarch to attach serious importance to annexing Scotland. His attempts could easily have been successful—bonds between southern Scotland and England were already quite strong—but the tyranny of Edward's agents touched that spark in the character of the Scot—the man with a great capacity for doggedness once he is angered—and the response was rebellion, the fires of which never cooled for centuries. The revolt, led first by William Wallace, who was executed, and later by Robert Bruce, ended in defeat for the English at Bannockburn in 1314.

Wallace and Bruce are hailed as the architects of Scotland's greatness. The daughter of Bruce married Walter, High Steward of Scotland. From this title came the name by which their descendants were known.

The spelling "Stuart", indicating Royal blood, was first used by Mary Queen of Scots; previously it was Stewart from the time of Robert II (1312-90), the first Stewart king. James IV

(1488-1513) who reigned for 25 years, the ablest of Scotland's kings, was the first Stewart strong enough to overcome the enormously disruptive influence of corrupt administration and feuding nobles, in both the Lowlands and the Highlands.

James brought the first real measure of prosperity to the country. But, with a foreign policy which was based on a long-standing alliance with France, he was forced to go to war with England when France, already at war with England, called on his help.

James was killed, with thousands of his men, on Flodden Field in 1513. The grand-daughter of James IV, Mary Queen of Scots, was one week old when she succeeded to the throne in 1542.

Brought up in the French court, a child bride of the French Dauphin at the age of six, she returned to Scotland a widow at 19, and was later forced to abdicate, fleeing to England and 19 years imprisonment there before her execution in 1587.

Her son, James VI, inherited the English Crown on the death of Elizabeth I in 1603, consolidating the movement towards each other of England and Scotland already perceptible with the Reformation.

Under the leadership of John Knox, Calvinism was established as Scotland's national religion in 1560.

Scotland kept her own separate Parliament for another 100 years. The union of the two Parliaments in 1707 was highly unpopular in Scotland, and distaste for the Union provided the driving force for the Jacobite risings of 1715 and 1745.

The second rising ended with the defeat of Prince Charles Edward Stuart, Bonnie Prince Charlie, at Culloden on April 16, 1746. It resulted in the repression of many Scottish institutions and deterioration of the clan system, setting the seal permanently on English government dominance.

It also had the totally unexpected effect of bringing a measure of popularity to the somewhat unprepossessing Hanoverian King George II: The meteoric success attending the first five months of the Catholic Prince's campaign touched unsuspected depths of patriotism in Protestant England. On September 28, 1745 the audience at Drury Lane Theatre heard a new Anthem, *God save the King.*

Today Scotland enjoys a considerable degree of regional government, with a Secretary of State responsible for a wide range of functions divided among a number of departmental ministers, assisted by a Minister of State and three Parliamentary Under-Secretaries and two Scottish Law Lords.

Four main departments of equal status (Agriculture and Fisheries; Development; Education; Home and Health) carry out their day-to-day administration in Edinburgh, but all have representatives in London.

The first man to preach Christianity in Scotland, St Ninian, was born in 350 AD near Whithorn, Wigtownshire. He gave his name to many of the wells (which the traveller still finds) where he is said to have blessed the water on his journeys through the country. They became places of pilgrimage for the sick.

St Columba came from Ireland and spent two years on the island of Iona from 563 AD, founding the abbey before undertaking a lengthy journey across the country, accompanied by some of his brethren. He converted the Pictish King Brude to Christianity.

The oldest Christian burial place in Scotland is St Oran's cemetery, Iona. The remains of 48 Scottish Kings, including those of Duncan, murdered in 1040 by Macbeth, are interred on Iona.

These strong links with the beginnings of Christianity and the early history of Scotland draw modern pilgrims who come to Iona by way of the beautiful island of Mull.

Survivors of some of the primeval animals which once roamed Scotland—brown bear, leaming, giant Irish Elk—are the roe deer and the red deer. They have learned to subsist without shelter, on bare hillsides, where once they would have had forests for protection and feeding grounds.

The last of the wolves is said to have been killed in Inverness-shire in mid-18th century. The saga of the wolf has importance.

Scotland had some of the most valuable ancient forests in the world, and burning them was one way of keeping down the wolves. The forests were burned, too, by Norse invaders and by skirmishing clans. Forests which survived to the 18th century were hacked down on the orders of army generals because they provided hiding places for retreating armies. In the 19th century the insatiable hunger for wood (for charcoal and smelting) of a growing industrial Britain swallowed as many of the remaining forests as profit-minded landlords and farmers cared to sell.

The chain reaction did not halt here for, with the valuable forests gone, landlords and farmers looked for other ways of making money and imported sheep from the Lowlands.

The coming of sheep to the Highlands was the culmination of a long, slow irreparable change in the landscape. Some of the remaining forests were burned to accommodate large flocks and thousands of men, women and children were driven from small crofts to make room for these animals.

In the mid-19th century many families chose to emigrate; others who remained were pushed to try to eke out a living on the poor soil of an exposed coastline.

This depopulation is something from which the Highlands have not yet fully recovered. Much has been done in recent years by the Highlands and Islands Development Board and by responsible farmers, landowners and business enterprises to redress the balance of that savage depopulation.

Hill land is being re-afforested, communities relying on fishing for a livelihood have been strengthened by scientific and financial aid, the population is slowly, but steadily increasing where means of new livelihood is being provided. Greater emphasis placed on research and the maintaining of a good balance between cattle, agriculture, and sheep has meant that some of Britain's great farming achievements in the past decade have been in this part of the country.

Scotland is still mainly agricultural in character with stock raising predominant and mainly large estates, where activities include grouse and red deer management.

Industrial expansion is a high national priority, particularly in the northern regions where it is perhaps most difficult for people to accept an industrial society and the idea of working in factories.

The Highlands and Islands Development Board is providing initiative and vitality. In some industries Scotland has at last ceased to be an outpost of Britain and become an important centre in its own right.

Successful growth of recently introduced outlets, especially electrical, electronics, and glass craft industries, has provided a momentum which if maintained will base the country's economy alongside the most technologically advanced in Western Europe. Economically this will offset to some extent the serious decline in shipbuilding and coal, and Scotland's ever-present problem of population drift.

Scotland's difficulties have no parallel in the rest of the United Kingdom. Distances have to be overcome. It is hard to attract suitable management, or keep promising trainees in remote areas, even when there is a good labour force available, particularly of women.

Scotland has to bring cohesion to an economy based on unusually diversified industries: the United Kingdom Atomic Energy Authority's £30 million prototype fast breeder reactor at Dounreay; seaweed factories; distilleries; cottage industries in the crofting townships; herring fleets; farms researching to redress years of lopsided husbandry; small coastal town boat builders; scattered islands dependent on one main source of livelihood, like the weaving of Harris tweed.

Traditional Scottish dishes owe little to sophisticated invention; they come from wholesome products of an abundant earth—salmon, trout, herring, oatcakes, shortbread, porridge, scones, Angus beef.

That special, subtly aromatic dish of ancient origin, the Haggis, is made from sheep's or calf's heart, liver, lungs, minced with oatmeal, onion, suet, spices, pepper and salt, and boiled in the animal's stomach.

Haggis is flown out to celebrations all over the world on January 25, Burns' Nicht, even to Russia where Scotland's National Bard is widely read and appreciated.

The whitewashed cottage in Alloway, Ayrshire, where the poet was born, is a tourist shrine and the vivid imagery of Tam o' Shanter is readily conjured up by the lush fields and burns of the surrounding countryside.

Of the many things that the Scots have given to the world, it would be a sweeping generalisation to say that *Auld Lang Syne* and whisky are perhaps the most international; this would ignore at least one incalculable contribution to international medicine—penicillin, the discovery of Ayrshire-born Sir Alexander Fleming.

Nevertheless "Scotch" has become a universal word, known in every bar in every part of the globe. Whisky was being distilled in Scotland at least 500 years ago, the first official mention of it appearing in the Scottish Exchequer Rolls of 1494 which read, "eight bolls of malt to Friar John Cor wherewith to make aquavitae".

The legal definition of Scotch Whisky is whisky made in Scotland, but such protection is no more than a formality because the pure air, crisp climate, moorland peat and, above all, the soft water from the Highland burns, give Scotch whisky an intangible individuality. The water is paramount above all other ingredients and distilleries are often sited in remote glens or unpolluted countryside near a swift-flowing burn.

Whisky is distilled chiefly from cereals (the Scottish penchant for thrift is advanced as the reason why farmers mashed their surplus barley, fermented and distilled it, producing the drink they called "water of life". It can be made from barley, maize and rye; this is the only ingredient where pedigree and environment do not matter. Barley from all over the world has been used by distillers with complete success.

There are two processes by which it can be distilled; the pot-still (producing malt whisky), which is the centuries-old method using only barley that has been "malted", or soaked and left to germinate; this is still the most popular method. The other process is by patent-still (producing grain whisky), the product of a mixture of unmalted barley and other cereals mashed with malted barley, a technique pioneered in the 19th century in Edinburgh which resulted in a new, milder blended whisky more suited to English palates at that time and, it transpired very quickly, more suited to the tastes of the rest of the world.

A tour of a distillery begins with the visitor watching the barley being soaked in the water from the burn. From this softening bath it goes to be spread on the floors of great, low-roofed halls, where it begins to germinate, a process which is stopped at just the right moment by being dried in a kiln.

It is in the drying that the barley absorbes the 'reek' from the peat fire. This aroma remains through all the varied chemical changes in the distilling process and perpetuates a mystery that has puzzled scientists for years.

About a month after being dried the barley is crushed before being taken to the cast iron mash tuns which measure 20ft across. In the tuns it is mixed with hot water so that the sugar in the barley is extracted, and then it is stored to ferment. Made of Oregon pine or larch, the tuns hold anything from 2,000 to 12,000 gallons of the sweet liquor to which has been added just the right amount of yeast.

Once the fermentation is complete—it takes about two days—the liquor is transferred to the wash still for its first distillation. Here the crude whisky is separated from the yeast and other unwanted matter before the alcohol, now known as 'low wines', is put into the neighbouring spirit still.

It is at this point that the stillman's experience and skill becomes of the utmost importance. The first part of the distillation and the last part—called the foreshots and the feints—are not considered of sufficiently high quality.

Therefore only the middle part of the distillation becomes whisky and the stillman's task is to decide the exact point in the process to let the spirit flow into the spirit receiver.

This is not the end of the process. From the spirit receiver, the clear liquid goes to be stored in oak casks. The casks must be of wood so that the spirit can "breathe" during the long years in the warehouse.

During this maturation period the spirit gradually mellows and takes on its characteristic golden hue—colour imparted from the casks, many of which have previously been used for storing sherry. Light-coloured whiskies are darkened by the addition of a minute quantity of colouring, stipulated by law, and consisting of caramelized sugar.

Few whiskies reach the market as 'straight' spirit. Nearly all are blends of malt and grain whiskies—usually about 50-50. The blender's nose is his most important instrument in this highly secret process and, to keep it in trim, he must never drink the product or smoke. Once the different whiskies have been poured together the blend is left alone so that the malt and grain marry.

Unlike the whisky, Scottish weather rarely gets its praises sung. There is a Scottish joke which says if it is clear enough to see to the other side of the loch it is going to rain, and if you cannot see to the other side of the loch it is raining already. June is generally the sunniest and driest month, particularly in the Highlands, while in central and east Scotland April can be a month of surprisingly low rainfall.

The traveller in Scotland finds one of its great attractions is the opportunity for a very wide range of outdoor activities. Nowhere is more than two hours from the sea by road. The deeply indented coastline, the thousands of freshwater lochs, the rivers, mountains, moors and forests, all constitute an ideal environment for active holidays: fishing, walking, gliding, skin diving, bird watching, and there are probably no finer places to sail than on the Clyde.

Scotland is the home of "Gowf", a game the Scots were playing before the *Mayflower* set sail for America. Golf, as it is now, is thought to have come from Holland; brought across to Scotland by traders at the time when commercial links flourished between the Netherlands and the ports of Eastern Scotland.

The Royal and Ancient Golf Club, at St Andrews, founded in 1754, is the game's ruling authority throughout the world. The Old Course at this club has written history which shows that it goes back to the 15th century, making it the oldest course in the world. It is still possible to play on it for a small fee. The low cost of golf is one of the outstanding features of Scotland, where over 350 excellent courses are listed, from sandy seaside courses with "billiard table" greens, to challenging hilly inland courses with daunting rough and superb views.

Long noted for its grouse shooting and deer stalking, the pattern of shooting has become commercialised and syndicated and changed as estates have become smaller—a growing population has had to be housed and provided with roads and factories—but there is still plenty of opportunity for the devotee.

From November to May winter sports enthusiasts converge on Aviemore, the Spey Valley resort, with good ski-slopes, ski schools, chair lift, tows, skating and curling rinks among its attractions.

Edinburgh, Scotland's capital, began with a few primitive Picts huddling on the Castle Rock. By 1385 their ancestors were still showing a hardy independence and a marked degree of 11 unexpectedness in behaviour. The English had just burned down the city; French troops came to Edinburgh's assistance; records report that the citizens "dyde murmure and grudge, and sayde, who the devyll hath sent for them? Cannot we maintain our warre with Englande well enough without their helpe?"

Edinburgh—"Mine own romantic town" Scott called it—is to its present citizens something more than a place of antiquity. It has all the panoply of a metropolis—offices, parks, gardens, a heavy concentration of traffic and a first-rate shopping centre.

With city boundaries which extend from the Firth of Forth at sea-level, to 1,500ft in the lovely Pentland Hills, it is a supremely sited city. It has been aptly described as "pure theatre". It clings to the side of hills topped by a mighty castle perched high on volcanic rock. There is a wide central thoroughfare with parallel gardens and 18th century Princes Street which divides the Old and the New Towns.

The Old Town is the one that evolved over the centuries winding its way higgledy-piggledy eastwards down from the castle to Holyroodhouse. This is the route of the Royal Mile and here are all the byegones to which every traveller turns first: The Castle Outlook Tower, Parliament House, City Chambers, Canon Gate, Tollbooth, the Palace of Holyroodhouse.

The Old Town took the brunt of wars and burnings. The wynds—narrow paths—which twist past ancient houses and shops are still there. There, to discover still, are the 17th century inn, the 15th century house, the 14th century church of St Giles, High Kirk of Edinburgh (known also as St Giles' Cathedral) where John Knox, preaching his fiery Calvinism, was hit by a stool thrown by an irate lady in the congregation.

The focal point of the Old City is the Mercat Cross, where 300 women died at the stake as witches, and where news was relayed of 10,000 deaths on Flodden Field. In one enclave, St Mary's Close which has now become part of the City Chambers, every inhabitant died of the plague; the Close remains much as it did at that time in 1645.

With the Union of the Scottish and English Parliaments the city expanded considerably. The 200-year-old New Town dates from 1767; it has the harmonic architectural elegance of the 18th and early 19th centuries, developed in a classic layout of Streets, Places, Crescents.

The capital's famous sons have mixed claims to fame. There is Sir Walter Scott who was born on August 15, 1771 in College Wynd, where Guthrie Street, just off Chambers Street, is today; and there is William Burke, body snatcher, hanged in 1829. Robert Louis Stevenson, an Edinburgh man, based his novel *Dr Jekyll and Mr Hyde* on the character of Deacon Brodie, an Edinburgh town councillor by day, a burglar by night. James Boswell, biographer of Dr Johnson, David Hume, philosopher, and Sir Henry Raeburn, whose 18th and 19th century portraits have left us a valuable record of the great people of his time, were Edinburgh men.

Two of Edinburgh's most renowned characters, Mary Queen of Scots, and John Knox, were not born in the city; but the violent clash between these personalities—Mary representing the old Catholic church and the Renaissance culture, and Knox representing the Reformation according to Calvin—influenced Scotland's capital and the history of the nation.

Glasgow is an industrial picture in a golden frame. On its doorstep lies Loch Lomond, the Campsie Fells, the Kilpatrick Hills, and the Trossachs. It is the third most populous city in Britain, weighed down with an impoverished legacy of massive architecture and out-moded decaying buildings. Its industries are those which were vital to Britain's 19th century expansion—coal, steel, iron, shipbuilding.

Impressive plans for the future could make Glasgow one of the pulsating cities of Europe, with good housing, the best road network in Britain, and more excellent shops added to the ones the city already has. The undertaking is formidable; if it is successful Glasgow will regain some of the prosperity it enjoyed when the riches of the New World poured into its new, expanding port in the 17th century.

The Glaswegian has the character-stamp born of a society used to sharing burdens; men who will not move if their backs are up: if this kind of man is annoyed he shows it; but he has great warmth and generosity of spirit.

The Highland gateway, Stirling, whose castle looms on a crag 250ft above the plain below, has dominated much of Scotland's history. It became a favourite royal residence, one of the most opulent castles in Scotland. Near its gates is the church of Holy Rude, where Mary Queen of Scots was crowned in 1543. This is the city the Highlanders will tell you has the first tang of the Highlands about it; the Lowlander might reply in retaliation that it is the last outpost of civilisation.

Stirling does not stand exclusively on its past; it has one of Scotland's most modern universities, with a superbly landscaped campus of the kind which is bringing British university design more into line with that of America.

Inverness, called "the capital of the Highlands", is an historic and attractive town lying along the banks of the River Ness in the Great Glen. The Great Glen, a geological fault which caused a long fissure, links Lochs Linnhe, Lochy, Oich and Ness to the Moray Firth, cutting a line of deep and beautiful valleys.

Inverness is not a large town, but it imprints itself on the memory because one has first to cross a spectacular wilderness to reach it, and, once there, it makes one of the best centres for touring the Highlands, or looking for the Loch Ness Monster.

Scores of people have testified to the existence of a Loch Ness Monster. Sightings have become more common since a main road was opened along the north shore in the thirties, but St Columba is said to have prevented a water beast from eating a Pict in the River Ness in 565 AD, and 14th century maps refer to strange phenomena bringing waves without wind to the Loch.

There are several photographs, all showing serpentine shapes, or large dark patches in the water, which so far defy scientific explanation. Among them are those taken by a London surgeon, another by a Scottish forestry worker who was familiar with the surroundings. Reports of the Monster's length vary from 30ft to 70ft, its colour from brown and grey to black, its texture smooth and snail-like, or scaly.

The Loch, plunging to 900ft, is inky black, too dark for research even with modern techniques. No one knows what caves might be at the bottom of the Loch, or what, if anything, lurks there. There is no scientific evidence of an invertebrate—which the Monster would have to be to fit all the descriptions—of this size ever having existed.

Its detractors dismiss it as bird formations, plankton, otters, even the wreck of a Zeppelin, but this does not stop the widespread interest and the occasional serious scientifically-mounted attempt to prove or disprove existence of the Loch Ness Monster.

Scotland has a rich store of folklore. Place names in ancient Norse and Gaelic take on new meaning from the legends that have grown round them with time.

One of the country's authorities, Otta Swire, in her books *The Inner Hebrides and their Legends* and *The Highlands and their Legends,* vividly awakens a world of myth: how the grave of Winter can still be seen on the Island of Mull, to which she was driven by Spring; the way in which the Fairy Flag of Dunvegan first came to the castle of the MacLeods in Skye.

The Gruagach Stone, where milk was left for the Gruagach ("long haired one"), a fairy who traditionally looked after cattle to prevent them falling into bogs or off the tops of rocks, can still be seen in some parts of the Hebrides. If the milk was forgotten the cows would yield no milk, or the cream would sink to the bottom.

The Lowland Brownie, who "emigrated" to the Islands, has a penchant for cleaning the house before the visitors arrive, and slapping people in the dark if they are not extremely neat and clean. Unfortunately he is not partial to sharing the house with dogs at night, and has 13 been said to kill the family pet if left indoors with the dog when everyone has gone to bed.

"Each Uisage", the Loch Ness Monster also has a place in Gaelic folklore. It is one of the terrifying water horses which lie in wait, not only in Loch Ness but in many of the dark lochs of the Highlands.

The Highland piper is as much part of Scotland's heritage as the many battles fought on Scottish soil throughout the centuries. In the days of the clan system every chieftain had his personal piper. The bagpipe is a wind instrument, making music through wooden reeds. The bag, an animal bladder, usually concealed in tartan cloth, acts as a wind reservoir, kept filled by a pipe from the player's mouth. The melody is played on the chanter, a wooden pipe with a double reed and finger holes. Three other pipes also emerge from the bag to rest on the piper's shoulders; these are the drones, providing bass notes as a simple harmony for the main tune played on the chanter.

The construction of the chanter allows pentatonic music to be played in three keys, G, D, and A. Much of the older bagpipe music is written in the key of G, suggesting that the chanter evolved from a simple pipe and that later generations discovered how to extend the musical range of the instrument by adding extra finger holes.

However, not all the art of Scotland is to be found in the bagpipes. There is a rich heritage of beautiful folk song, remarkable both in verve and pathos. The songs of the Highlands and Islands, expecially the Hebrides, are full of the poetic imagery of the Celts. The Lowland songs, closer to the English, have left us with some of the world's most memorable ballads, including *Annie Laurie.*

Soon after the end of World War II Edinburgh inaugurated a three-week season of music, drama and art which has become world famous as the Edinburgh International Festival. Renowned orchestras, drama groups, choirs, composers and instrumentalists take part. Special exhibitions of painting and art are staged to coincide with the event, held during the last two weeks of August and the first week in September. Not since the 18th and 19th centuries, the time when Scotland provided the heart for the great Romantic Movement which swept Europe, have the artistic energies of the Scottish capital been infused with so much vigour.

Organisations have had to be formed (Scots Ancestry Research Society, the Scottish Tartans Information Society) to keep everyone, not just the Scots, informed about those Scottish institutions, the clans and their tartans.

Today's clans exist as societies where people bearing the same name gather socially. Loyalty is still strong, there is tremendous feeling of comradeship between people who, although not related by blood in anything but the remotest possible way, share the same Scottish name. "Clan" simply means "children" and the system had the outline of its beginnings three thousand years ago with the Picts and the Irish Gaels.

Apart from Albania in eastern Europe, Scotland is the only country today in which such a family system survives. Indeed, Scotland's ancient name was Alba, and the two countries, Albania and Scotland, wear the kilt as national dress, organize their families in the same way and have several other features in common.

Tartan was certainly used by the clans as far back as the 12th and 13th centuries.

In August, 1538, a record was made in an account book for three ells (an ell measures 37 inches) of "heiland tartan to make the King's Grace's trews", and even earlier, in 1471, the court treasurer wrote "halve an elne of doble tartane to lyne ridin collars to her lady the Queen" (the Queen was Margaret, wife of James III).

Tartans began as badges of rank. The system developed from families living in the isolated glens. Not having much contact with neighbouring families—except when fighting—they evolved their own rank system, from the all-powerful chief to the youngest ghillie. Every single member of the clan was fanatically loyal to the chief. Tartans later became badges of districts and finally badges of clans.

By 1710 most clans wore a distinguishing tartan, and tartans with their great variety of colour and pattern, became a ready means of identification; the weavers of one clan never wove tartan for another, even when the population of a village was mixed.

The man who revived interest in the tartans was Sir Walter Scott when he arranged that famous and spectacular all-Scottish, all-tartan welcome to King George IV to Edinburgh in 1822. The King attended a ball at the Palace of Holyroodhouse wearing full Highland regalia and pink silk tights.

Over the years since then tartans of every clan—and an unknown number of imitations—have been used for dress and furnishing materials, ties, caps, car seat covers, carpets, and bathing costumes among an endless range of products.

The kilt has formed the main part of the dress of the Highlander from the early part of the 17th century, although there is evidence that this too is very much older. There were actually two kilts, the "breacan-feile" or belted kilt, and the "feile-beag" or little kilt.

The wearer of the former had to be a pretty patient man when dressing, for the twelve ells of tartan had to be folded about him to show the set (pattern). Half of the material formed the kilt and half was slung over the back to form the plaid, the garment being fixed at the waist by a stout belt and the plaid to the shoulder by a brooch.

The "feile-beag" was the model of the kilt as it is worn today; made of six ells of tartan, it was pleated and sewn and fixed at the waist by small straps, leaving half a yard at each end to cross each other at the front.

The demise of the kilt as the natural dress of the Highland Scots came in 1746 when, after their defeat at the battle of Culloden, the Hanoverian Government proscribed wearing of the garment. Anyone caught wearing it was imprisoned for six months on his first offence and deported for seven years if caught again. It was not until 1782 that the Highland Scots were permitted to wear the kilt again, but by this time many of the original setts were lost and weavers had to rely on people's memories. Today's setts are not always strictly those which distinguished the originals, and many are 19th and 20th century inventions.

The last decade with the growing ease of global travel has brought a greater demand for tartan than ever before. One of the things many a first-time visitor to Scotland does is to find a shop that sells tartan and ask if his name has even the remotest connection with a clan. Most of the shops have a thick book of names—it is astonishing what obscure links can be found to gratify this international love of tartan.

Foreign names, however unlikely they may sound, are often shown to have tenuous connections with a Scottish name.

A dyed-in-the-wool Sassenach is persuaded that because he bears allegiance to his sovereign who is descended from the House of Stuart, there is a tartan for him.

An utterly lost soul, with no claim whatever, can as a last resort choose a tartan simply because it appeals to him—and tell himself that he is helping the export trade.

Margaret Hides

The statue of Allan Ramsay, 18th century Scottish poet, overlooked by one of the most famous castles in the world.

Edinburgh Castle, possibly on the site of an Iron Age fort, has been a stronghold from time immemorial. The rock on which it stands was used as a refuge and habitation when the first primitive Picts huddled together there. It served as a barrier against north and south as long ago as the seventh century, and the rebuilding of a castle on this site is recorded from that time.

Reliable records from the 11th century show that Malcolm III and his Queen, Margaret, made the castle their residence, and the oldest part of the present cluster of buildings which make up the castle is the 11th century Queen Margaret Chapel.

The ancient city grew in a downhill straggle between the Castle and the Palace of Holyroodhouse.

The 16th century Great Hall, now an armoury, has an exceptionally fine hammerbeam roof. Below the Hall, prisoners of the Napoleonic wars were kept in vaulted rooms, many of them carved their names, or pictures of gallows and ships on the doors. The Castle holds the Scottish National War Memorial, opened in 1927. There is also the Old Palace where Mary Queen of Scots gave birth to James VI (later James I of England).

Outside the walls, on Castle Hill, is the Outlook Tower whose Camera Obscura throws a bird's eye view of the city on to a table.

The Castle battlements look down on the Esplanade where the military tattoo is staged in late August and early September during the Edinburgh International Festival.

The Palace of Holyroodhouse, Edinburgh, the official residence of the Queen in Scotland, on the site of what was once a modest guesthouse for the ancient Abbey of Holyrood.

Used now only occasionally by the Queen it was made into a Palace at the beginning of the 16th century by James IV, and enlarged and reconstructed by the architect Sir William Bruce for Charles II.

Steeped in the tragic history of the Stuarts, visitors to the Palace can see the private apartments of Mary Queen of Scots and the audience chamber where John Knox, leader of the Protestant Reformation in Scotland, whose writings include his *First Blast of the Trumpet against the Monstrous Regiment of Women* was received by the Catholic Queen. The Palace of Holyroodhouse was the home of Mary for six years from 1561. On a night in March 1566 the pregnant Queen, forced to stand at sword point and see her secretary, David Rizzio, stabbed to death, was told she would be cut into collops if she moved. Her husband Darnley was strangled less than a year later at his house at Kirk o' Field. The house, which stood on the site of the present University, was blown up the same night.

Visitors to the Palace can also look through the window from which Mary's infant son was lowered to safety in a basket to protect him from his mother's enemies.

In 1603 James received the news that he had become monarch of the two kingdoms when a messenger, riding from the death-bed of Elizabeth I in Richmond Palace, Surrey, completed the 400-mile journey to Holyroodhouse in 62 hours.

The ill-fated Prince Charles Edward Stuart held brief court here in 1745.

Early in the 19th century when Britain was having a love affair with the novels of Sir Walter Scott and all things Scottish, George IV visiting Holyroodhouse attended a ball wearing pink silk tights with full Highland regalia.

In that border region which is a mixture of hills, fishing harbours, woods and ancient abbeys the ruins of Tantallon Castle command a magnificent position on the rocky coast of the Firth of Forth, opposite the Bass Rock.

This 14th century stronghold, washed on three sides by the sea, protected on its landward side by a double moat, is three miles north east of Berwick. It was persistently besieged by James V in 1528, but not until 1651 was it eventually destroyed by General Monk.

The Firth of Forth, cutting between Edinburgh and Dunfermline is spanned by the new Forth Road Bridge, which was opened by the Queen on September 4th 1964.

The bridge has taken the place of boats which for centuries provided the main link between the two cities—the ferry ceased on the day the bridge was opened.

The cost of building the bridge with its network of toll-road approaches, footpaths and cycle tracks, was £20,000,000. Its two main towers are 512ft high, its central span 3,300ft long.

Although envisaged as long ago as 1923 the bridge was not started until 1958 after it had been finally decided that a bridge, and not a tunnel, would make the link.

For six years a construction team of 350 men worked to complete it.

A short way down the river is the cantilevered Forth Railway Bridge, completed in 1880: each bridge an engineering wonder of its time.

24

Jedburgh Abbey, even as a ruin remains one of the most memorable buildings of Scotland.

Founded in 1118 it stood for 400 years before being burned down on the orders of the Earl of Surrey in 1523.

The restored Norman tower, and an interesting museum which was once a house where Mary Queen of Scots stayed, make it well worth a pause on The Borders.

Craigievar Castle, near Alford, completed in 1626 has no later additions and is one of the loveliest castles in Scotland.

Bought by the National Trust for Scotland in 1963 the inside has some outstanding examples of richly moulded plaster ceilings, particularly in the Great Hall, where the plaster relief of the Royal Coat of Arms is very fine.

Its tower stands alone, its conical roofs, turrets and crow-stepped gables, corbelling and balustrading contrasting sharply with the more austere lines of the rest of the out-side of the building.

Melrose Abbey on The Borders. Built in the 12th century for Cistercian monks it came under repeated attacks in border wars and was finally destroyed in English raids in 1544.

The best that remains is in the chancel, transepts and nave.

The novelist Sir Walter Scott spent most of his later life near Melrose in a mansion at Abbotsford two miles away. He drew much of his inspiration from the surrounding Border country. His study is preserved as he left it, visitors see the desk at which many of his best-known novels were written, and a romantic collection of miscellania including the sword given by Montrose to Charles I, Prince Charlie's hunting knives, and Queen Mary's seal.

The novelist is buried in the ruins of Dryburgh Abbey, five miles south-east of Melrose.

Seen together from Erskine Bridge—Dumbarton, gateway to lovely Loch Lomond, and the tremendous beauty of Scotland that lies along its shores; and the River Clyde, symbolic of the country's tradition of great ocean liners and industrious hard work.

Roman Bridge, Loch Trool, nestling in the 135,000 acre Glen Trool Forest Park of Kirkcudbright.

32

Kames Castle, Port Bannatyne on the little island of Bute, which with Arran and other adjacent islands forms the county of Bute. Bute lies off the Cowal peninsula separated by the beautiful stretch of water known as the Kyles of Bute. It is 16 miles long, and no more than a few miles wide, and it has an interesting mixture of scenery from the hilly north to the flatter, more fertile, south. Its major town, Rothesay, a Clyde resort and steamer port, is the town from which the Prince of Wales takes the honorary title Duke of Rothesay.

*Amid all the provinces of Scotland,
if an intelligent stranger were asked
to describe the most varied and most
beautiful, it is probable he would
name the county of Perth.*
    Walter Scott, *The Fair Maid of Perth.*

This Perth landscape is near Loch Kinardochy.

36

Loch Tay, in Gaelic Loch Tatha—peaceful, or still lake—is one of the finest salmon fishing waters in Britain. Fish as heavy as 50 lbs have been taken on this loch with the rod.

The loch stretches for almost 17 miles. From the eastern end the River Tay flows 120 miles to the North Sea, and at the head of the river is the pretty village of Kenmore where in 1787, at the Breadalbane Arms Hotel, Robert Burns wrote, in pencil over the parlour chimney, a poetic description of the beauty surrounding Loch Tay.

At the opposite end of the Loch, Killin, with its famous falls, is a great tourist attraction, and the whole region offers excellent facilities for holiday walking, climbing or motoring in the surrounding hills.

The curious, lowering attractiveness of Easdale is not immediately apparent because the first impact is grey, stony and sparse, but the water is crystal clear, a few boats often add colour, and there is friendliness towards the visitor.

Slate grey rocks, forming a natural breakwater, and long grey-green headlands, thrust into the Sound of Insh and beyond into the Firth of Lorne along Scotland's south-west shores. Low purple hills lie opposite Easdale, and waves can prance capriciously between them, hammering on the many outcrops of rock on less calm days.

40

Easdale, Isle of Seil, not a pretty-pretty village, but strangely compelling with houses, most of them kept smart and attractively coloured, providing sometimes-needed cheerful contrast to the dark scree hills which come down on two sides of Easdale.

42

Glencoe, scenery to touch the spirit, is one of Scotland's wildest and most celebrated glens, which goes from Loch Leven to Rannoch Moor.

An unbelievably audacious sweep of hills and moors tempts you to believe they have the whole planet to themselves.

There are fast, clear rivers, with beds of rounded stones in white, pink, brown and grey; and little tarns so blue that nobody believes you when you recall them.

Glencoe, the glen of weeping, was the scene of a brutal massacre in 1692 when a company of soldiers, under a Campbell commander, massacred 40 MacDonalds who had been their hosts for nearly two weeks. The Campbells rose at 5am and in the middle of a snowstorm began the slaughter. The chief of the Macdonalds was murdered, a monument to him stands near the entrance to the glen.

The A82 road takes in the full length of Glencoe's memorable beauty and then continues through equally awesome scenery as far as Killin.

Inveraray Castle has been the seat of the chiefs of Clan Campbell, Dukes of Argyll, for centuries.

The castle, on the shores of Loch Fyne, has the River Aray running through its pleasant ornamental grounds.

Started in 1743 the present castle is one of the earliest examples of Gothic revival, and for a time the Adams family, father and sons, were involved in the work.

The exceptionally fine interior has portraits by Raeburn, Ramsay, and Gainsborough as well as many historic relics.

All the colour and majesty of the West Highlands is evoked in Glencoe's Loch Trioch-
atan, where the grey-green on lower slopes
becomes bare and sparse towards the top,
finally petering out into a slaty blue.

Endless moors, sometimes narrowly pinched
between towering hills, add a spectrum of
greens to this glen, and drifts of colour come
at all times of the year with wild flowers,
particularly in the early Autumn when
heather spreads for miles.

Glencoe takes its name from the River Coe
and an untamed stream which rises in the
hills.

Mountain Rescue Vehicles, always part of
the Glencoe scene, remind you that this can
be tough, inhospitable country for the fool-
48   hardy.

View from McCaig's Folly, an unfinished replica of the Colosseum in Rome, built by Stuart McCaig, a banker, as a memorial to his family in 1890.

He started it to relieve unemployment in the area at that time and to provide a museum for the town.

It tops a headland overlooking Oban, a delightful town which has come to be known as the holiday capital of the Western Highlands. Certainly in the summer there is a distinct holiday air here: yachts, their sails puffed, hustle importantly to and fro in the nooks and crannies off shore; the ferries for Mull are crowded; the shops in town selling tweed and tourist souvenirs do a roaring trade.

But after the holiday season is past there is calm among the hills, green and wooded, which are an integral part of Oban and the surrounding countryside.

Claimed to be the only bridge to 'span the Atlantic' Clachan Bridge, Seil Sound, carries on its incredibly high hump-back the narrow road which turns Seil Island into a short peninsula linked to the mainland 15 miles south of Oban.

The bridge was designed in 1793 by Thomas Telford, Scotland's renowned engineer, whose technical masterpiece is the Caledonian Canal.

Loch Linnhe, with Stalker Castle on its tiny island, exchanges this pastoral setting as the hills begin to ridge back in layers and the water broadens until it becomes a seascape taking in larger and larger islands and joining the Firth of Lorne on Scotland's south-west coast of Argyll.

54

Loch Morlich with a backdrop of the Cairn-gorms, those granite peaks which provide some of the most testing climbing in Britain, and link Inverness-shire, Aberdeen-shire and Banffshire.

The Cairngorm ski runs: classified into grades—easy, intermediate and skilful—provide British winter sports enthusiasts with their best conditions on home ground. The mountains take their name from the easily accessible Cairn Gorm, although at 4,084ft it is neither the highest, nor the most dramatic, of the chain which includes Cairn Toul (4,241ft), Ben Macdhui (4,296 ft), Braeriach (4,248ft). With the exception of Ben Nevis they form the highest peaks in the British Isles.

Weather moods can change swiftly, from brilliant sun to wisping mists and rain, from snow in winter to perilously freezing conditions.

The mountains, rich in rare flora, are the home of eagle, ptarmigan, wildcats and deer.

Loch Morlich, at an altitude of 1,046ft is a beautiful inland loch set among silver birch and pine forests where deer roam. Little remains of the great forest of Rothiemurchus which once spread along its shores. The 100 sq mile Cairngorm National Nature Reserve, the largest in Britain, provides some of the most splendid scenery in the country, majestically mingling waters, hills, forests, moorlands.

One of the most spectacular, though not always easy, routes for walkers is the 20 miles along the Pass of Lairig Ghru which links the Dee and Spey Valleys.

The Castle of the Comyns—13th century rival contenders for the throne of Scotland. From fortresses like this on Loch an Eilean, and Ruthven, the 14th century Wolf of Badenoch, notorious brother of Scotland's Robert II, reigned terror on the countryside. This land of warrior clans, transformed into a peaceful natural holiday area, offers walks through extensive forests and along rivers and lochs, and the best winter sports facilities in Britain.

After an absence of 70 years ospreys have recently returned to nest in this district.

A few miles north, at Carrbridge is the newly opened centre of Landmark—the first interpretive visitor centre in Europe showing in sound, vision, landscaping, flora and fauna, how man has survived and evolved in these surroundings.

The visitor to Landmark is transported back 3,000 years and hears the Arctic winds whistling overhead; he sees lynx, bear, beaver, wolf and wild boar roaming this country; watches Government Redcoats patrolling these hills, and clans rustling each other's cattle. He has opportunity to grind his own oatmeal with a hand quern, or imagine himself preaching Christianity to the Northern Picts.

Landmark evokes what life was like in the Highlands when every roof was thatched and the Castle of the Comyns kept guard.

Crinan stands at the western end of the Crinan Canal, nine miles long, completed in 1801 to save ships a 120-mile voyage from Loch Fyne to the Atlantic.

But statistics, whatever engineering feat they represent, will never do justice to Crinan.

The road into this little haven runs alongside the canal and its locks, getting more and more beautiful as it reaches towards Crinan. A lighthouse tops a headland, there is an impact of colour—green hills, aquamarine water, painted houses, yachts, pleasure boats and the more sombre hues of honest-to-goodness fishing boats and their tackle. Bronze Age stone circles in the vicinity and several castles make Crinan worth a diversion in the time schedule of even the most pushed traveller.

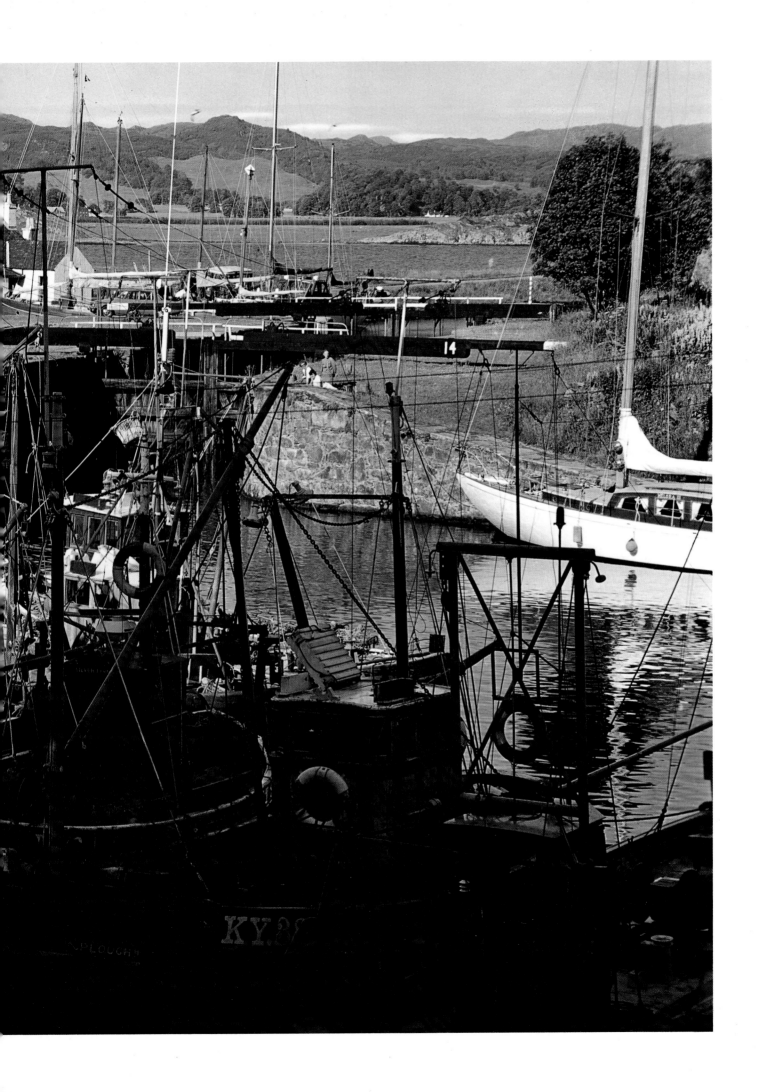

The Road to the Isles. On the way to Morar
and Mallaig travellers pass the Glenfinnan
Monument of a kilted Highlander at the
head of Loch Shiel, near the spot where
Prince Charles Edward Stuart, Bonnie
Prince Charlie, first raised his standard in
Scotland on August 19th 1745 as a rallying
point for the clans.

The monument, erected in 1815, commem-
orates the clansmen who fought and died
for the Prince's lost cause.

"Land of the bens and glens and the heroes" is how Gaelic poets describe the country where this farm stands on the edge of Loch Ailort, Arisaig, in Scotland's largest county —Inverness-shire.

Ruffle through a list of place names and you come up with much of the history of the Highlands: Culloden, Glencoe, Lochaber, Glenfinnan, Ardnamurchan.

It is said that Macbeth died in a castle on Loch Lundarva, that St Columba passed through on his way to Inverness.

There are the lofty crags of the Cairngorms, and there is Ben Nevis, Scotland's highest mountain which dominates the major township of Fort William.

Another sight to be remembered in Inverness-shire is Loch Ness with its vast length and its depth in some places up to 900ft.

Loch Eilt—the Road to the Isles. Arisaig,
Inverness.

The haunt of Golden Eagle, and the hunting ground of Wildcat and Pine Marten is not far from this stretch of the River Ghairbhe, Kinlochewe.

West of Kinlochewe, at the head of Loch Maree, the Beinn Eighe National Nature Reserve, the first in Britain, founded in 1951, covers more than 10,000 acres. Primeval Caledonian pines survive, and red deer roam freely over the hills.

Commanding the confluence of Loch Alsh, Loch Long and Loch Duich is the 13th century Castle of Eilean Donan, near Dornie, a castle which has stood against many sieges.

Like many of the numerous castles in the Highlands it has had a stormy past since the Middle Ages.

In 1590 Donald Gorm MacDonald, chief of his clan, sailed across the strait from Skye with his war galleys to capture the castle. He was hit in the leg by an arrow and in temper tore the arrow roughly by the shaft, almost severing an artery. He was carried to his war galley and brought to a little isle rising out of the water within sight of the castle where his men tended him until he died from loss of blood.

In 1719, defended in the cause of Jacobite sympathisers by Spanish mercenaries, it was bombarded by the English warship *Worcester*.

It was renovated in 1932 and is now a clan war memorial.

If Wester Ross had nothing to show but Loch Maree it would be worth the journey to the far north of Scotland.

One of the most beautiful inland lochs, it is surrounded by hills and wild splendour; some of the finest woodland in the country lies along its shores.

Druids worshipped on Isle of Maree, one of the minute islands dotted in its waters.

And there is more to this part of the country: gorges, waterfalls, ancient forests, hushed glens; it has a grandeur and solitude which some people find too remote and overwhelming.

. . . the coming of sheep to the Highlands was the culmination of a long, slow, irreparable change in the landscape.

Sheep shearing near Loch Maree, Ross and Cromarty. Scotland had some of the most valuable ancient forests in the world. But over the centuries these were denuded to a point of extinction—burned by Norse invaders and in skirmishing by local clans; hacked down by armies in search of enemies in hiding; sold off for charcoal and the growing industrial needs of 19th century Britain.

Sheep offered a new source of profit to farmers and landlords who burned some of the remaining forests to accommodate large flocks, and cleared thousands of men, women and children from small crofts to make room for the animals.

In the mid-19th century many families chose to emigrate, others who remained were pushed to try and eke out a living on the poor soil of an exposed coastline.

Much has been done in recent years by the Highlands and Islands Development Board and by responsible farmers, landowners and business enterprises to redress the balance of that tragic depopulation of the Highlands. Hill land is being re-afforested, the population is slowly increasing where means of a new livelihood is being provided. Greater emphasis placed on research and the maintaining of a good balance between cattle—the original husbandry of the Highlands—agriculture and sheep has meant that some of Britain's important farming achievements in the past decade have been in this part of the country.

74

Loch Rosque in Achnasheen's remote magnificence where the roads to Kyle of Lochalsh and Skye part from the route to Loch Maree and Torridon.

76

Ullapool, situated on Baden Bay, has its streets named in Gaelic and English. It has become a leading centre for sea angling, and big game fishing for sharks. Long established as an important herring fishing port, and also as a popular holiday town, it makes an unrivalled centre for exploring the glorious scenery of the North West Highlands.

The old bridge at Sligachan and Cuillin Hills, Isle of Skye.

Skye has been the guardian of Scotland's history for 4,000 years. At each turn the traveller encounters tales of warriors and heroes, of myths and magic; while demanding attention all the time is some of the most spectacular scenery in the Highlands.

It was to Skye that Bonnie Prince Charlie fled as a fugitive from the English troops under the Duke of Cumberland after the Battle of Culloden in 1746.

Disguised as Betty Burke, a servant, the Prince landed at Kilbride while accompanied by Flora MacDonald from Benbecula; the next day, June 30th, he bade farewell to her at Portree, later embarking on a ship which was waiting to take him to France.

Much of the island's countryside remains as the Prince must have seen it. The Cuillins dominate the south of the islands. Good roads link most places; it is only in the interior that roads are poor and, in Knoydart— a district "lying between heaven and hell" —where there are virtually no roads at all, the coast dwellers turn to boats as the only sensible means of transport.

Visitors to Skye can see the grave of Flora MacDonald at Kilmuir and Dunvegan Castle, stronghold of the MacLeods of Skye who have lived here for 700 years.

Sango Bay, near Sutherland's crofting township of Durness, remains genuinely Gaelic and has become a very pleasant holiday centre for tourists and fishermen.

Not far from Sango Bay are the Caves of Smoo, popular with sightseers. The caves consist of two chambers, the first is about 200ft long and 120ft high and is easily accessible; the second, less accessible cave, has an 80ft waterfall cascading into it.

In summer a minibus meeting the ferry across the Kyle of Durness gives visitors an opportunity to see the massive and isolated cliffs of nearby Cape Wrath, the extreme north-west point of the Scottish mainland. It was from this point that the Viking invaders turned south en route for the Hebrides which they held for 400 years, until the 13th century.

Loch Eriboll: In the tranquillity of Northern
Sutherland the caves of Loch Eriboll provide one of the few mainland breeding
grounds for the grey seal in the British Isles.
Remote and often uninhabited islands provide most of the other breeding grounds.

86   Loch Bervie Harbour, Sutherland.

From the Scottish borders to the islands of Shetland, Scotland is an angler's paradise. Loch Assynt is noted for salmon and brown trout.

Scotland, long famous for salmon and trout fishing, also offers excellent sea angling off her extensive and beautiful coast, as well as good opportunities for coarse fishing for pike, roach and grayling.

Sometimes referred to as Scotland's Matterhorn, the 2,309ft Suilven—near Lochinver, in Sutherland—is the country's most remarkable mountain. It rears from undulating surroundings like some strangely shaped prehistoric monster.

Its dangerous cliff faces were formed from a sandstone-layer-on-top-of-rocks formation more than two and a half million years ago. The rounded top is known as Casteal Liath (grey castle), Suilven means pillar, best appreciated if you see it from its west side. Its slopes are more gentle on the eastern side. But the northern and southern aspects present the most formidably precipitous face.

90

Loch Cairnbown and the Quinag hills in the infinite of Sutherland, the most sparsely populated county in Britain. Fewer than seven people per square mile live here, compared with the average of 586 for Britain as a whole.

Some of the most spectacular scenery in the British Isles waits for those who don't equate sparseness with harshness in these remote Highlands on the road to nowhere.

Where the high hills come down to the plains in a mingling of swift salmon rivers and quiet lochs, lush farmland grazed by Highland cattle, and sandy beaches. Where pine forests encroach to the edge of heather moors; and where working ports are never far from castles—fairy-tale conical-towered castles, over 150 of them—here you will find the Old Bridge of Dee, Invercauld.

Here too you will find the Queen's summer home, the holiday castle of Balmoral. And in September you could attend the Braemar Royal Highland Gathering.

This is where Scotland's history catches up with the traveller along every mile of the road.

The onset of Autumn in leaf-green, purple
and soft gold-brown: colours which blanket
Scotland at this time of year.
This is a quiet stretch of the River Dee near
Ballater, a busy resort on Royal Deeside.
Early Autumn and late Spring are often the
best times of year for good weather in
Scotland.

The sea fishing industry, falling into three main divisions—white fish, shellfish and herring—is specially important to Scotland's economy.

Aberdeen, Scotland's third largest city, is one of Scotland's chief centres for white fish.

Aberdeen, often called the Granite City because of the stone used for its buildings, has a long history, recorded as far back as the 12th century. It was here, in the 13th century, that Robert the Bruce campaigned against his rivals for the throne, the Comyns.

One of the oldest inhabited houses in Scotland, 10th century Traquair House, Innerleithen, Peebles.

The house, containing valuable embroideries, silver, glass, tapestries, some of it from the 13th century, has been the home, or played host to more than 25 Scottish and English monarchs.

William The Lion, 12th century Scottish King held court here. In 1566 Mary Queen of Scots stayed at Traquair and the house contains several relics of Mary.

In the rebellion of 1745 Bonnie Prince Charlie stayed here. It is among the claimants to be the original Tully-Veolan of Sir Walter Scott's *Waverley*.

Since the 18th century strong ale has been a tradition of Traquair House. The unique brewhouse, still in full working order, which brewed ale for the staff and estate tenants, is in production today and using the 200-year-old copper to make ale which is bottled and sold to visitors.

A stronghold of the Earls Marischal of Scotland from the 14th century, the impressive ruins of Dunnottar Castle, just south of Stonehaven, Kincardine, tower on rocky cliffs 160 ft above the sea.

It was here that the Scottish Regalia was brought for safety during the Commonwealth wars only to have to be hurriedly smuggled out by the wife of the minister of nearby Kinneff, and hidden under the pulpit of the church, when Cromwell's troops entered and occupied the castle in 1652.

Part of this treasure, some of it dating from the 14th century, can now be seen in Edinburgh Castle. It includes the Scottish Crown Jewels which are older than those in the Tower of London.

The Cathedral at St Andrews, Fife, once the largest church in the country with a length of 391ft. King Robert the Bruce attended its dedication.

St Andrews, ancient university city of immense charm, was the ecclesiastical capital of Scotland, and some of the most savage fighting and destruction of the Reformation took place within the city's walls. In June 1559 an unruly mob stripped the Cathedral of its sculptures and ornaments, and by 1649 the townsfolk were allowed to help themselves to its stones for any building purpose they liked.

Little remains now apart from sections of the south transept and choir, most of the surviving work belongs to the late 12th and 13th centuries.

The Cathedral precincts, enclosed by a high wall almost a mile in length, covered about thirty acres, and the gaunt skeleton of the once-lovely building looks over the east end of the city, and down towards the cliffs and harbours.

Crail, whose Royal Charter, dating back to 1310, gave it the right to trade on the Sabbath—a custom which later upholders of the Reformation had a job to stamp out after John Knox preached one of his inflammatory sermons in the Collegiate church in the summer of 1559.

However, Crail's shops are back in business on Sundays and it has grown into a favourite holiday resort while at the same time remaining a genuine work-a-day fishing port.

It is the farthest east of the little fishing villages on Fife's East Neuk rocky coast. The lobster creels piled high on the harbour have been made here for generations, and in the season lobsters from Crail are dispatched each day to the fish markets of Britain.

On the wide tree-lined Marketgate, the Town Hall, with a Dutch tower, reflects the influence of the Continent when Crail was a major Scottish port.

The Collegiate church has an 8th century Pictish cross slab.

The red weathered tiled roofs of the old stone houses make an enchanting picture as they cling in higgledy-piggledy fashion to steeply shelving roads going down to the water's edge. They were once the haunt of smugglers. Many of them now belong to artists, and some come under the care and protection of the National Trust for Scotland. No golfer coming here should miss a visit to Balcomie Links, an 18-hole course beautifully sited at the edge of the sea.

Crathes Castle, whose double square tower dates from 1553, is one of the finest castles open to visitors in north-east Scotland.

Its story goes back more than 650 years. The Lands of the Leys were granted to the Burnett family here in 1323 by Robert the Bruce, and among the castle treasures on show is the richly jewelled Horn of Leys presented by the King.

But probably the greatest glories of Crathes are its Chamber of the Nine Nobles, The Green Lady's Room, and the Chamber of the Nine Muses, with ceilings which were painted in 1599.

110 Loch Feochan, Argyll, at sunset.